SPECTRUM®
READERS

MYSTERIOUS!
Outer Space

By Katharine Kenah

Carson-Dellosa
Publishing

An imprint of Carson-Dellosa Publishing, LLC
P.O. Box 35665
Greensboro, NC 27425-5665

carsondellosa.com

The publisher would like to thank the NOAA Photo Library, NOAA
Central Library; OAR/ERL/National Severe Storms Laboratory (NSSL)
for their permission to reproduce their photograph used on the cover
and title page of this publication.

ISBN 978-1-62399-153-1

01-002131120

Most people wake
up with the Sun.
They go to sleep
looking at the Moon.

Every day, the sky affects
our lives in big and small ways.
Turn the page and step outside.
The mysteries of space are
waiting for you!

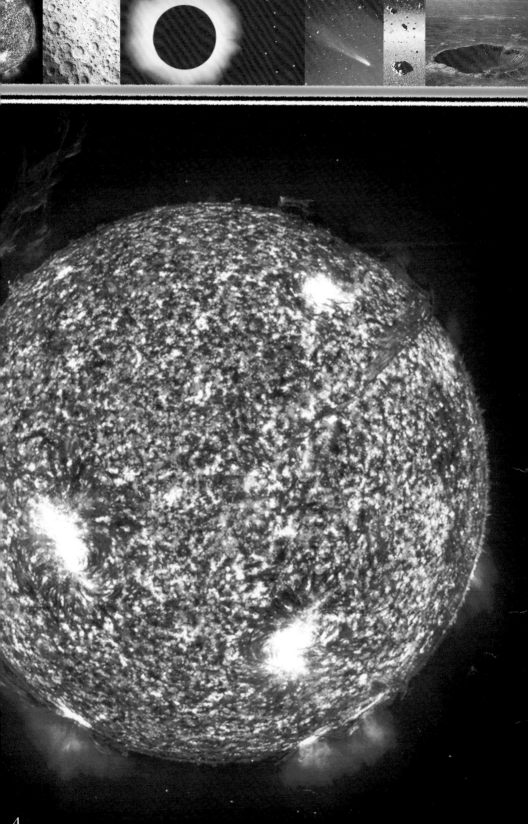

Sun

The Sun is not a big star.
It is not a small star.
It is just an average-sized star.
But it is the star closest to Earth.

The Sun is a ball of hot, burning gas.
It sends heat, light, and energy
to people, plants, and animals.
There would be no life on Earth
without the Sun.

Weird Facts

- The temperature at the Sun's center is 26 million degrees.
- The Sun is 110 times larger than Earth.

Moon

The Moon is Earth's
closest neighbor in space.
It is made of rock.
The Moon has no weather,
no wind, and no water.

The Moon is the brightest light
in the night sky.
But the Moon makes
no light of its own.
Moonlight is sunlight that
bounces off the Moon!

Weird Facts

- Moon dust is made of ground rock and glass.

- If Earth were the size of a basketball, the Moon would be the size of a tennis ball.

Eclipse

Earth circles the Sun.
The Moon circles Earth.

Sometimes, the Moon passes
between the Sun and Earth.
The light of the Sun
is hidden by the Moon.
This is called a *solar eclipse*.

Sometimes, Earth passes
between the Sun and the Moon.
Earth's shadow covers the moon.
This is called a *lunar eclipse*.

Weird Facts

- A solar eclipse can be seen only in places where the Moon's shadow covers the ground.

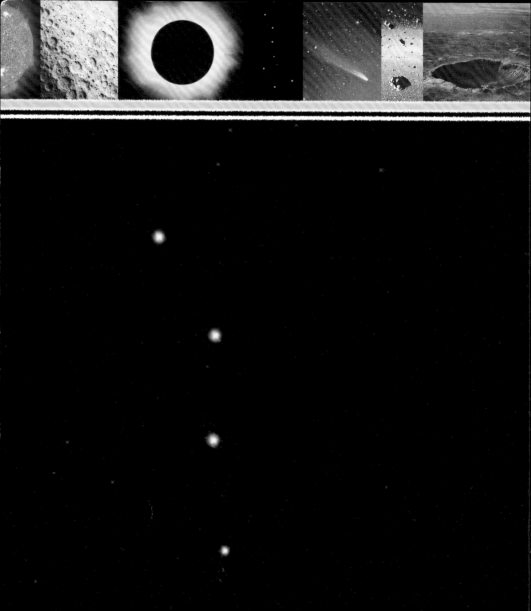

Constellations

Some stars form pictures
or shapes in the night sky.
These groups of stars
are called *constellations*.
Constellations are named for animals,
people in myths, and everyday things.

Weird Facts

- The Big Dipper looks like a soup ladle.
  The two stars at the far end of the ladle
  point to the North Star.

- The North Star, or the Polaris Star, is
  right above the North Pole.

Comet

A comet is like a giant,
dirty snowball.
It is more than a mile wide.
A comet is made of dust,
rocks, gas, and ice.

Comets move around the Sun.
The Sun's heat melts some
of the comet's icy outside.
Dust and gas fly out into space.
This forms the comet's bright tail.

Weird Facts

- Halley's Comet is a comet that appears in the sky every 76 years. It was named after Edmund Halley.

- Shooting stars are bits of comet dust and ice falling into Earth's atmosphere.

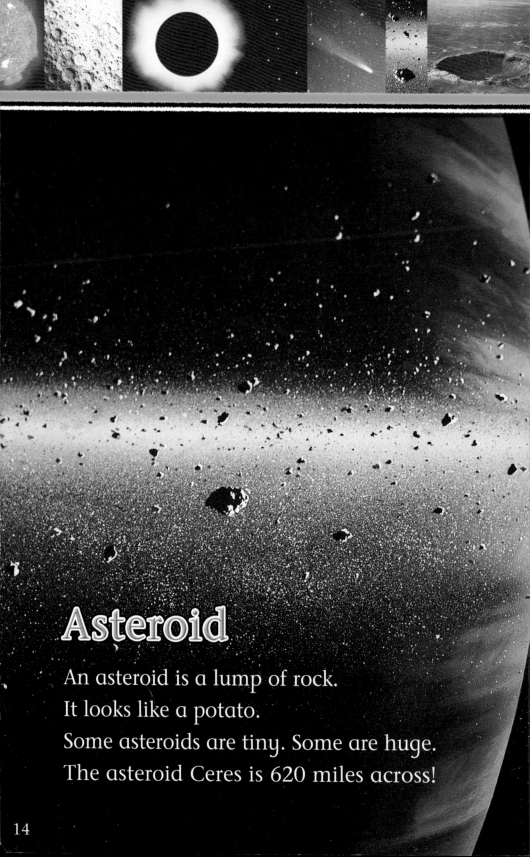

Asteroid

An asteroid is a lump of rock.
It looks like a potato.
Some asteroids are tiny. Some are huge.
The asteroid Ceres is 620 miles across!

Most asteroids move around the Sun
between Mars and Jupiter.
This area is called the *asteroid belt*.
Asteroids are as old as the solar system.
They may be pieces of planets
that never formed.

Weird Facts

- Asteroids are full of valuable metals, such as nickel and iron. Mining companies are working on ways to mine these metals in space!

- Near Earth Asteroids are asteroids that pass close to Earth. A collision with these asteroids could cause disaster.

Meteoroids

Small objects falling through space
are called *meteoroids*.

Meteoroids are made of bits of rock
from crashing asteroids.

They are also made of dust
falling from comets.

When meteoroids hit the air around Earth, they get hot and glow! These streaks of lights are called *meteors*. If a meteoroid lands on Earth, it is called a *meteorite*.

Weird Facts

- Some people think that a meteorite crash 65 million years ago may have killed the dinosaurs on Earth.

- 50,000 years ago, a million-ton meteorite hit Arizona. It made a bowl-shaped dent in the ground. The crater is 570 feet deep and nearly a mile wide!

Milky Way

The Milky Way is a galaxy.
A galaxy is a group of stars
spinning in space.
Every star in the universe is in a galaxy.

The Milky Way is shaped
like a pinwheel. It is made of
billions of stars, dust clouds, and gas.
Our solar system is just one small part
of this huge galaxy.

Weird Facts

- The Milky Way is shaped like a pancake with a thick center and thin edges.

- The Milky Way has dark spots that look like holes. They are really just dust clouds that hide the stars behind them.

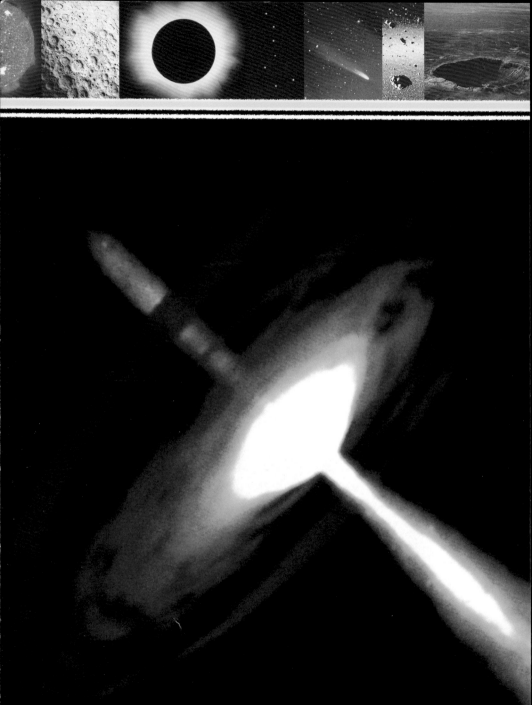

Black Hole

This is not a top spinning in space.
It is a black hole!

When people jump into the air, a force
called *gravity* pulls them back down.
A black hole is a spot in space
where gravity is very strong!
A black hole pulls everything into it.
Nothing can escape it, not even light.

Weird Facts

- A black hole cannot be seen by the human eye.
- Temperatures near the edge of a black hole rise close to 180 million degrees!

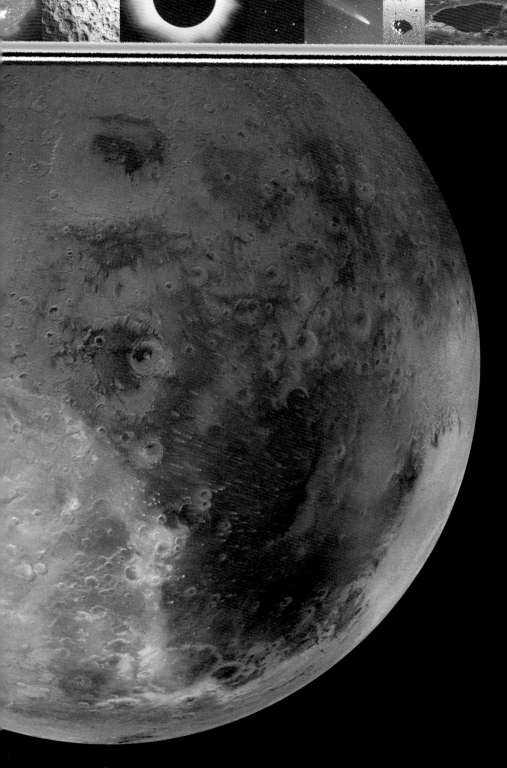

Mars

Mars is called the *Red Planet*.
Mars' red color comes from
the iron in its soil.
Mars has mountains, deserts,
canyons, and polar ice caps just like Earth.
But Mars has no water to drink
and no oxygen to breathe.
Huge wind and dust storms
whirl around Mars.

Weird Facts

- Mars has weaker gravity than Earth. If you weighed 100 pounds on Earth, you'd weigh 40 pounds on Mars.

- Mars got its name from the god of war in ancient myths.

Saturn

Saturn is the second largest planet
in our solar system.
It is full of liquid.
This makes Saturn very light.
It would float on water!

Saturn has seven rings.
Saturn's rings are made of
chunks of rock and ice.
These chunks can be as small as
snowflakes or as big as houses!

Weird Facts

- Saturn has "shepherd moons." These
moons keep chunks of rock and ice in the
rings from straying out of place, just like
a shepherd keeps sheep together.

Dwarf and Giant Stars

A star lives in space for
millions of years. It shines
until it runs out of fuel.
Then, the star starts to swell.
It grows to 30 times its normal size.
This is called a *red giant*.

Then, the star puffs out gas and dust.
It starts to shrink.
All that is left is the star's
tiny, hot center.
This is called a *white dwarf*.

Weird Facts

The planetary nebula, or glowing part, of
a dying star sometimes becomes part of
a new star!

Northern Lights

Something is shimmering
in the sky. It looks like
a dancing curtain of lights.
Is it lightning? Is it a fire?
No! It is the northern lights.

Sometimes, small bits of gas
fly off from the Sun in streams.
They hit the air around Earth
and start to glow!
This is called the *northern lights*.

Weird Facts

- In the northern hemisphere, the northern lights are called the *aurora borealis*. In the southern hemisphere, they are called the *aurora australis*.

29

Sky Watching

When the Sun goes down,
sky watchers go outside.
Some people use telescopes.
Some people use binoculars.
Some people go to planetariums
to watch star shows.
Some people simply
use their own eyes.

Look carefully. The mysteries
of space are everywhere!

Weird Facts

- Ancient astronomers thought that the stars traveled around Earth.

- Laika was the first dog to explore space! Laika traveled into space in 1957 on board the Sputnik 2 satellite.

MYSTERIOUS! Outer Space Comprehension Questions

1. What star is closest to Earth?

2. Why do you think there would be no life on Earth without the Sun?

3. What is the moon made of? What is moonlight?

4. What is the difference between a solar eclipse and a lunar eclipse?

5. What are constellations? How are constellations named?

6. What is a comet made of?

7. Where is the asteroid belt? How big is the asteroid Ceres?

8. What are meteoroids made of? What is it called if a meteoroid lands on Earth?

9. Why do you think Mars is called the *Red Planet*?

10. How many rings does Saturn have? What are the rings made of?

11. Why do you think some people enjoy sky watching? Do you think it is something you would like to try?